the work of frei otto

Ludwig Glaeser

the work of frei otto

The Museum of Modern Art, New York
Distributed by New York Graphic Society Ltd., Greenwich, Connecticut

Copyright © 1972 by The Museum of Modern Art

All rights reserved

Library of Congress Catalog Card Number 75-150084

Cloth Binding ISBN 0-87070-332-3

Paperbound ISBN 0-87070-333-1

The Museum of Modern Art
11 West 53 Street, New York, N.Y. 10019

Printed in the United States of America

Photograph Credits

Architectural Forum, New York, 39, 48
Cosmo, New York, 126 top right, 126 bottom left
Fritz Dressler, Stuttgart, 62, 63, 64, 65, 114 top, 114 center
Ludwig Glaeser, New York, 70, 71
Office of Rolf Gutbrod, Berlin, 59
Edward Hord and Douglas Tachi, Washington, D. C., 126 bottom right
Institut für leichte Flächentragwerke (Institute for Light Surface Structures), Stuttgart, 14, 15, 17, 20, 25, 26, 28, 33, 34, 35, 36, 40 bottom, 42, 45, 47, 53, 57, 75, 76, 77, 85, 86, 91, 96, 102
Herman Kendel, Berlin, 111
Lutz Kleinhans, Frankfurt, 72, 73, 74
Richard Larry Medlin, St. Louis, 49, 50
Osamu Murai, Tokyo, 60, 61, top
Frei Otto, Stuttgart, 13, 16, 18 bottom, 19, 21, 22, 23, 24, 27, 29, 30, 31, 32, 36-37, 37, 40, 41, 43, 44, 46, 54-55, 56, 58, 61 bottom, 67, 68, 69, 79, 80, 81, 82, 83, 84, 87, 89, 90, 92, 93, 97, 98, 100, 101, 107, 113, 116, 117, 118, 120, 121
Conrad Roland, Berlin, 94, 95, 98-99
Ezra Stoller, Mamaroneck, N. Y., 126 top left, 127
L. Stromeyer and Company, Konstanz, 52
Swiss National Tourist Office, New York, 18, top
Wilkinson Studios Ltd., Montreal, 51

Drawings (redrawn from material provided by Frei Otto and the Institute for Light Surface Structures, Stuttgart), Daniel de Pol, New York

The computer-drawn elevation, page 112, produced by Klaus Linkwitz, Geodetic Institute, University of Stuttgart

1661960

Contents

Acknowledgments

This publication is based on an exhibition shown on the Garden Terrace of The Museum of Modern Art from July 7 to October 4, 1971. During the extended period of preparation, both the exhibition and the publication received help and encouragement from many sides. First of all, I wish to thank Frei Otto who not only gave his consent to the project but also his full support in raising the necessary funds as well as in providing the requested material. These were generously supplemented by Conrad Roland, author of the first publication on Frei Otto, which proved invaluable as a reference source. Berthold Burkhardt at the University Institute for Light Surface Structures, Stuttgart, supplied and verified the data on many of the projects.

Much is owed also to the dedication of those involved in the realization of the project. Mary Jane Lightbown handled the complex research and contributed to every phase of its organization and execution. Harriet Schoenholz Bee edited the various texts for the exhibition and publication with exemplary patience. Gai Moseley was involved in every aspect of the design, and supervised its execution.

The Foreign Office of the Federal Republic of Germany provided a grant, which in part subsidized this publication. I wish to thank, in particular, Haide Russell, Consul for Cultural Affairs in New York, for her continuous support.

The project could not have been realized without funds contributed by various individual and corporate donors. I am deeply grateful for their generosity, and especially for that of Mrs. Douglas Auchincloss, Armand Bartos, Bruce Graham, Philip Johnson, and Phyllis Lambert, which has benefited architecture on numerous previous occasions. This is particularly true of John Entenza, who during the last decade as Director of The Graham Foundation has, with cognizance and courage, come to the rescue of many an otherwise lost cause.

Ludwig Glaeser

Introduction

Frei Otto is concerned with the fundamentals of structure. In pursuing the age-old question of all construction—how to achieve more with less, that is, less material and effort—he has elevated the traditional tent to a modern building type capable of remarkably large spans. Frei Otto believes in modern technology, and, from the beginning, envisioned structures of extreme lightness as well as extreme strength, which were to make optimum use of new materials such as thin cables of high-strength steel or thin membranes of synthetic fabric. He also saw the potential of pneumatically distended membranes, the only building type considered suitable for extraterrestrial conditions.

During the millenia in which man had to rely on gravity to give buildings stability, the enormous amounts of material used were disproportionate to the actual loads that vaults and domes had to carry. Even in modern shell structures the dead weight of a dome equals most superimposed loads. Frei Otto arrived at solutions that, for the the first time, reversed this ratio.

He developed his new concepts by focusing his investigations on one of the principal forces extant in all structural systems—tensile stress. Because the nature of most construction materials involves only compression forces and the concomitant bending and buckling moments, it is insignificant in conventional buildings. The reverse is the case with tensile structures where only a few members, such as masts, are under compression while all others, such as cables and membranes, are under tension. In order to introduce tension and to ensure rigidity, membranes must have specific shapes, which in most cases are based on anticlastic or saddle-like curvatures. Furthermore, these curvatures can, if correctly determined, generate the smallest possible surfaces within given curvilinear boundaries. These observations led Frei Otto, after years of experimental and analytical studies, to formulate his theory of minimal surfaces.

Frei Otto's achievements and their prerequisite dedication to a single idea cannot escape biographical interpretation. Born in 1925, the son and grandson of sculptors, he was initiated in the stonemason's craft but spent most of his free hours inventing and building model planes. Later, flying glider planes, he had his first opportunity to observe the behavior of thin membranes stretched over light frames and exposed to aerodynamic forces. Drafted into the German Air Force, he served as a pilot during the Second World War. In a prison camp at Chartres he was put in charge of a reconstruction crew attempting to repair bridges and buildings without any construction materials. His methodical ingenuity led Frei Otto to structural solutions which, he discovered later as a student, were not common engineering practice but genuine innovations.

Frei Otto returned to Berlin in 1947 and started to study architecture at the Technical University. While the faculty offered only one outstanding teacher of structural analysis, it was an exchange visit to the United States in 1950 which determined his future preoccupation. Among the architects he met was Eero Saarinen who recognized Frei Otto's deeper interests and referred him to Fred Severud. The renowned civil engineer was at the time involved in the State Fair Arena at Raleigh which, designed by Matthew Nowicki was the first large suspension roof to be built. After his return, Frei Otto not only produced a similar scheme, a concert hall with a suspended roof, but the year after his graduation in 1952, wrote a doctoral thesis on suspended roofs.

In the following years, he carried out his research from load-stabilized suspension structures to prestressed tensile systems. His theoretical work was paralleled by executed structures progressing from simple to more complex forms in ever larger spans—the result of his increased knowledge and of the continuing feedback provided by the experimental studies which accompanied each project.

As singular as Frei Otto's present position may appear, it nevertheless is rooted in the architectural development of the postwar period. The need to regain and reassert an interrupted tradition was soon satisfied to the extent that the modern idiom became universal practice. At the same time, modern architecture's founder generation was unable to prevent the institutionalization of its concepts and faced increasing criticism from its disciples in the early 1950s. Denouncing dogmatism in favor of more pluralistic solutions, Eero Saarinen wrote "The Six Broad Currents of Modern Architecture," which was published in the July 1953 issue of *Architectural Forum* and subsequently translated into German by Frei Otto. CIAM (Congrès Internationaux d'Architecture Moderne) conferences had been the forum of the dissidents but, under their attack, ceased to convene at the end of the 1950s. Even its long-time secretary, the historian Sigfried Giedion, pronounced heretic views in "The Need for Imagination," which appeared in the February 1954 issue of *Architectural Record.* Looking for a resurgence of communal spirit, he regarded the new shell structures as capable not only of roofing enormous assembly halls but also of expressing the emotional aspirations of our civilization. However premature this postulate, one cannot deny that these light vaults and domes were the most important architectural events of these years. Not surprisingly, most of them were the contributions of engineers like the Mexican shell builder, Felix Candela, one of his colleagues Frei Otto admires most. Lack of distance still blocks the historical assessment of these trends but indicative of their significance, however, are the identical solutions produced by architects who were quite independent and distant from each other. In Frei Otto's work there are two such coincidences in one year: the Entrance Arch at the 1957 Horticultural Exhibition in Cologne, which employs the same formula of an arch-supported saddle roof as Eero Saarinen's Yale Hockey Rink completed the following year; and the Dance Pavilion at the Cologne Exhibition which displays a star-shaped arrangement of undulating surfaces similar to Felix Candela's restaurant in Xochimilco, completed in 1958. Intrigued by the sculptural potential of these new construction methods, Le Corbusier designed an outright tensile structure, the Philips Pavilion at the Brussels World's Fair in 1958.

Most of the shapes employed in shell and membrane structures, such as hyperbolic paraboloids, seem without precedent in modern architecture, which has always aimed at a reduction to elementary geometric forms. Yet, as is evident in the work of the Constructivists, there was, early in this century, a persistent tendency to explore more complex geometries. More accessible to sculptural realizations, they became the exclusive theme for artists like Naum Gabo and Antoine Pevsner, whose curved surface segments are often compared to three-dimensional translations of trigonometric equations.

Their work, however, exerted no direct influence on Frei Otto who names Constantin Brancusi as the sculptor he admires most for excellence of craftsmanship as well as inventiveness of plastic forms. By admitting his interest in analyzing Brancusi's surfaces scientifically, he confirms his own attitude toward sculpture as that of an observer. Similarly, he observes the forms he finds in nature, which in their origin and efficacy are even more relevant to his theories. He regularly holds seminars at which biologists discuss their research on plant and animal structures. Besides such obvious adaptations as the "vertebrae column," his methods themselves have a tendency to produce forms which, for instance in the "tree" structures or space frames, are of outstandingly organic character. Frei Otto does not deny the sculptural quality of his work but maintains that the forms are nothing but physical manifestations of the laws that govern the nature of materials and that they remain unattainable to anyone who attempts to produce these forms in an exclusively subjective manner.

Therefore, it is justifiable to say that Frei Otto approaches form from the knowledge of structure rather than the love of sculpture, and his denial of artistic motivations is believable to the extent that he avoids burdening a project from the outset with preconceived ideas. But since he admits to a personal style in problem solving, his forms are not totally automatic results of the design process. However scientific the methods, there is a margin for personal decisions which accounts for the individual style discernible in the work of most engineers.

Since the beginning of the modern movement, architects have admired engineering structures for their geometric purity and monumental scale. Frei Otto's involvement is more direct and marked by an intuitive understanding of the physical properties of structure. His solutions are distinguished by simplicity and conceived like those of most great engineers as direct-force systems. His design approach, however, reveals yet another trait—inexhaustible curiosity. For a single project Frei Otto produces innumerable system sketches until he has covered all theoretical aspects of the given structural type. In a parallel approach, he strives to exhaust all practical applications suggested by analytical examination. In many respects, Frei Otto shows less the characteristics of the planning architect or the calculating engineer than the speculative mind of the inventor. Nothing illustrates this as well as the many mechanical details he has designed, which range from cable clamps for tents to measuring devices for models.

Since most of his structures are not only statically indeterminate but also defy two-dimensional representation in conventional drawings, models obviously had to become his principle tool. Part of an integrated process, they are built and rebuilt in different materials and at different scales, from delicate soap-film models used to verify minimal surfaces to solid wood models for wind-tunnel tests. They are the means for establishing the formal configuration of the surfaces as well as for conducting the statical analysis in which adjustable models equipped with special measuring devices, such as strain gauges, simulate actual stress conditions. With the aid of an automated three-dimensional measuring scaffold, topographical surveys are made of the surfaces, and data for drawings is transmitted to a computer. While models are rarely made for presentation purposes, they serve Frei Otto as didactic tools to explain the structural system to others as well as to himself. Finally, ideas materialize in models, such as a series of catenary vaults and domes which he developed simply by reversing the patterns of hanging chains or nets. On the other hand, Frei Otto's constant use of models is not without disadvantages in that their three-dimensional concrete presence reinforces the sculptural rather than the spatial quality of his forms.

Frei Otto, who has worked only as a consultant since he gave up practicing architecture in 1970, contends he always lacked the confidence that one could still make architecture in our time. Many will agree to the extent that at least the way in which architecture has been made can hardly provide solutions for today's tasks. The ongoing transformation of building practice from craft execution to mass production alone can cause such a demand for research that it will change architectural offices into industrial laboratories. Frei Otto recognized the inevitability of the situation in 1957 when he founded, on his own, the Development Center for Lightweight Construction in Berlin. It was succeeded in 1964 by the Institute for Light Surface Structures which the University of Stuttgart established for Frei Otto as a research and teaching facility. Complete with staff, students, and an array of sophisticated instruments, the Institute afforded him a unique opportunity to test his theories on large-scale projects. For the last three years, housed under a membrane roof originally built as the test structure for the German Pavilion in Montreal, the Institute has operated most informally within its open environment. Groups assemble and disperse according to projects, while individuals can isolate themselves by plugging their heating and seating units into the pipe system at the point of their preference. The same informality pervades the think-tank operations as well as the study programs which benefit equally from Frei Otto's ability to discuss problems with as much patience as enthusiasm.

Frei Otto, who sees himself primarily as someone who stimulates others, likes to point out that most of his work has been carried out with changing groups of collaborators. The range of his personal contribution is indeed difficult to determine: it can be limited to the role of consultant, but in most cases it affects all aspects of the design process. While he emphasizes his dependence on the help of others, Frei Otto has at the same time a remarkable facility for assembling and coordinating large-scale operations involving industrial corporations, government agencies, architectural firms, and consulting experts, all from different countries. His working methods also reflect the experience he has gained from many years of close collaboration with industrial firms, in particular with the Stromeyer Company in Konstanz. The firm, one of the world's largest tent manufacturers, was enlightened enough to support his research from the beginning, and has now become the leading producer of tensile membrane structures.

Frei Otto's theory of minimal structures has been summarized as an attempt to achieve, through maximum efficiency of structure and materials, optimum utilization of the available construction energy. As a consequence he sees the architect less as a designer than as a manager of this energy, which is the sum total of material and labor involved in construction. However, economy was not the only objective in developing lightweight systems; freeing architecture from its structural and material re-strictions means to Frei Otto making it more liveable for man. Thus the reduction in construction elements yields increased flexibility and allows the adjustment of interior spaces according to the changing needs of the occupants. At the same time, tensile structures, which are easily expanded and transformed, also provide external adaptability, not only to specific site conditions but to environmental requirements in general. The facility with which these structures can be erected, dismantled, and transported offers further advantages for increasingly mobile societies.

Frei Otto not only considers the temporary nature of his membrane structures desirable but admits that his objections to making architecture stem from his reluctance to fill the earth's surface with lasting buildings. He hesitates to pursue a project unless he is certain that its realization will be temporary enough not to be in man's way. This endorsement of obsolescence contradicts the traditional view of architecture as a fulfillment of man's need for monuments. Yet, as vernacular buildings of all periods prove, artistic value is not dependent on the durability of a structure, nor on the amount or preciousness of its material. On the other hand, temporariness does not mean improvisation, as is evident from the amount of research invested in each lightweight structure.

Frei Otto acknowledges that current scientific methods have advanced only far enough to deal with elements of structure and to guarantee perfection in buildings that exclude the human element, such as an automated factory. Since the decisive factor in the design process, in his opinion, is the analysis of the problem, he believes that progress depends on new analytical methods. The predicaments such a new science faces are the innumerable nonobjective factors that enter building as well as any other human activity. He is aware that they must be accommodated if scientific criteria are to succeed in re-establishing the primacy of human needs.

Illustrations

Mast and Cable Supported Membranes

Frei Otto's extensive research in the field of mast and cable supported membranes launched his theories of minimal structures. Most of his executed structures belong to this category, and, however modest in scale, they provided indispensable technical experience and demonstrated the remarkable potential of lightweight systems.

The first of Frei Otto's tensile structures to be built, the Bandstand in Kassel of 1955, is the prototypical anticlastic or saddle-shape solution. The membrane is supported at two opposite points by poles and anchored at two opposite points to the ground. Peaked tents, where simple saddle surfaces are supported at one point, are a variation of this type, the most spectacular examples of which are the pavilions of the Swiss National Exhibition in Lausanne, 1964. By means of supporting and restraining ridges, saddle shapes were employed additively resulting in a variety of undulating tents. Extremely sculptural, this tent type included three of the most impressive structures Frei Otto ever designed—the star-shaped Dance Pavilion in Cologne of 1957, and Wave Hall and the Small Pavilions in Hamburg in 1963. While these ridge-type membranes were supported at various points by poles, Frei Otto introduced a continuous support in the form of a thin steel arch in the Entrance Arch at Cologne. The last major type, membranes with high points or with high and low points, used enlarged mast heads, which gave such structures as the second shelter tent at Cologne the characteristic humped appearance.

Bandstand, Kassel. 1955

13

Shelter Pavilion, Cologne. 1957

14

Exhibition Pavilions, Lausanne. 1964

16

Exhibition Pavilions, Lausanne. 1964

Dance Pavilion, Cologne. 1957 (above and following page)

Hangar Tents. 1957 (above and preceding page)

Wave Hall, Hamburg. 1963

Wave Hall, Hamburg. 1963

24

Small Pavilions, Hamburg. 1963

26

Small Pavilions, Hamburg. 1963

Entrance Arch, Cologne. 1957

Open-Air Theater, Wunsiedel. 1962–1970

Humped Pavilion, Cologne. 1957

Interbau Café, Berlin. 1957

34

1661960

Exhibition Hall, Berlin. 1957

Membrane Hall, Hamburg. 1963

Large-Scale Projects

From the mid-1960s on, Frei Otto received an increasing number of commissions for large-scale projects, which allowed him to prove the actual advantages of tensile structures. Large spans can be bridged more economically by tensile structures than by any other system. The reason is not only that most materials have a greater strength under tension than in compression, but also that the length of tensile members can be increased considerably without increasing their volume proportionally. The imperatives of large spans, however, affected the sculptural quality and variety of forms typical of most of Frei Otto's smaller structures. Thus the necessity to minimize the wind pressure on large surfaces demanded low-curved forms. Simple saddle shapes were employed only in composite or additive arrangements, while arch-supported structures and variations of the high-point type were more effectively adapted to large-scale use. Frei Otto designed membranes to cover an entire dock in Bremen or a construction site for six-story houses in a London suburb, huge conical structures with one central support to roof a medical academy in Ulm or a conference center in Riyadh. Most recently he designed, in collaboration with Kenzo Tange, giant arch-supported cable nets that will shade the Sports Center arenas in Kuwait. The only executed example of a large-scale structure, his German Pavilion at Expo '67 in Montreal, afforded Frei Otto with invaluable experiences from design procedures to erection methods. Another large project, transparent membrane elements which—in a continuous arrangement — cover the Olympic Stadia in Munich, is now under construction.

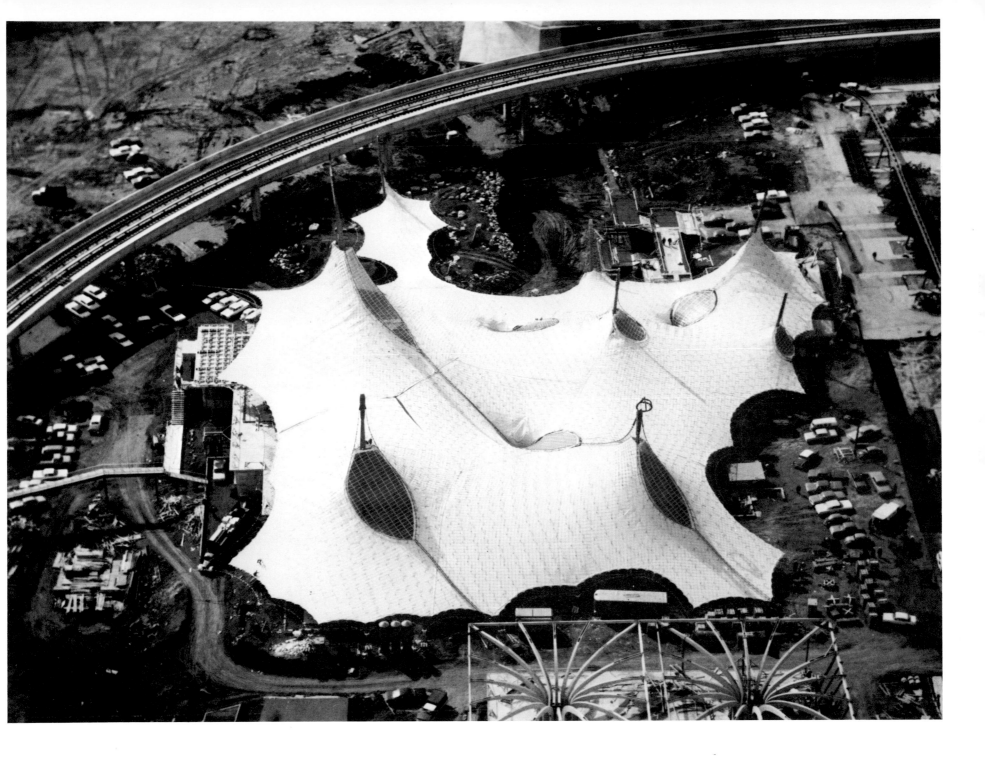

German Pavilion, Montreal. 1967

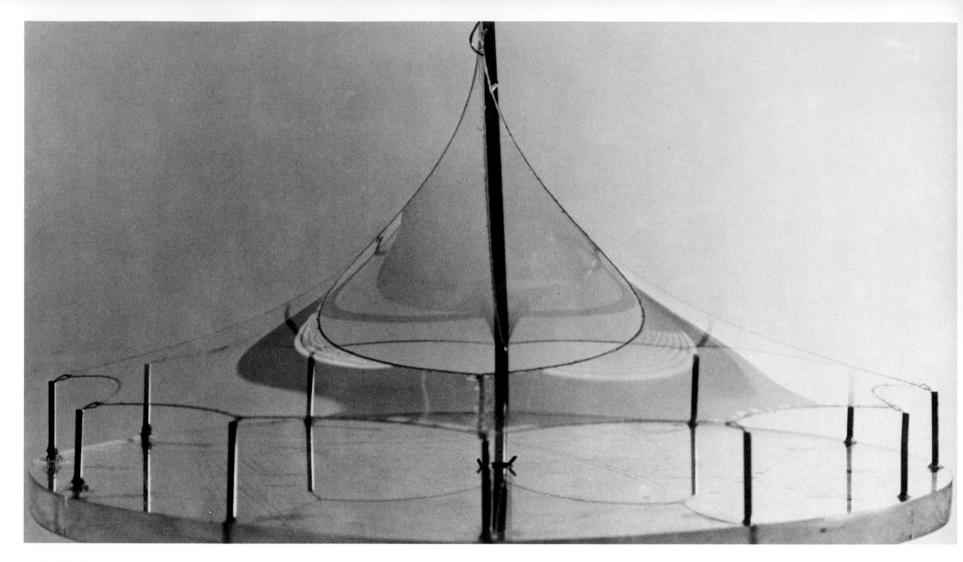

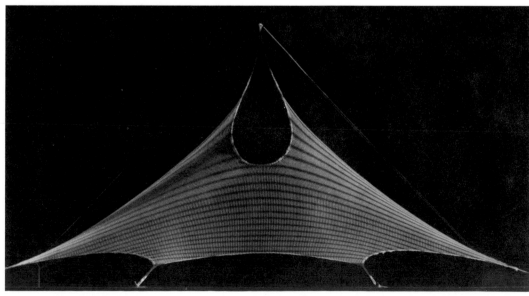

German Pavilion, Montreal. 1967 (Study models)

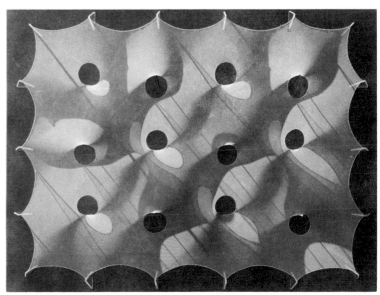

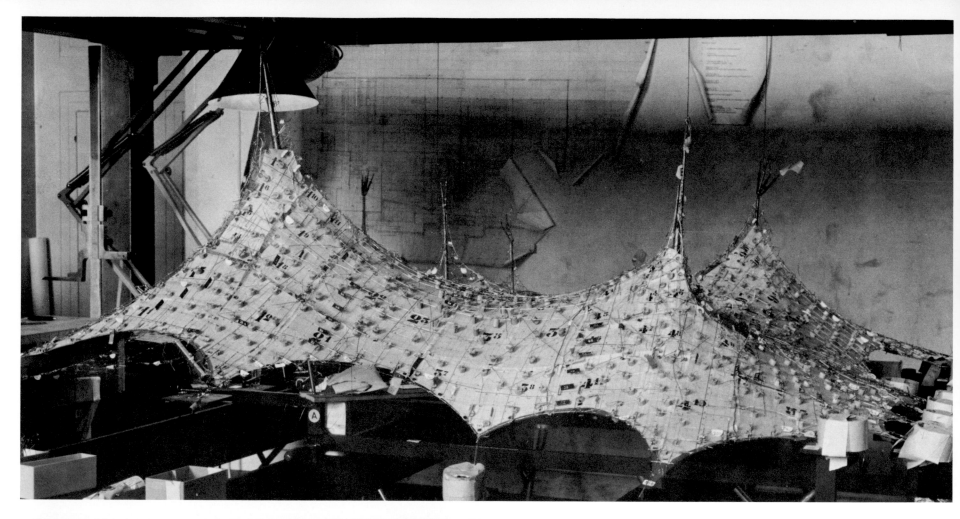

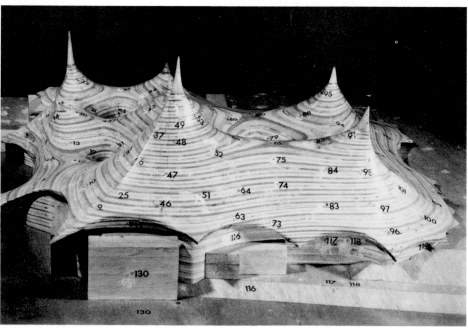

German Pavilion, Montreal. 1967 (Measuring and wind-tunnel test models)

German Pavilion, Montreal. 1967

German Pavilion, Montreal. 1967

German Pavilion, Montreal. 1967

46

German Pavilion, Montreal. 1967

German Pavilion, Montreal. 1967

German Pavilion, Montreal, 1967

Dock Cover, Bremen. Project 1961

54

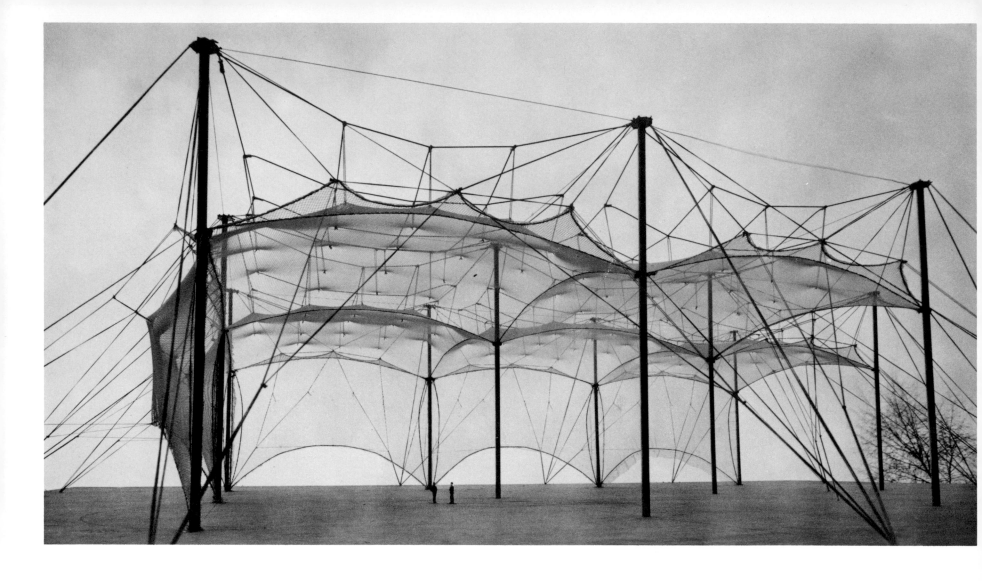

Construction Site Cover, London. Project 1965

Indian Pavilion, Osaka. Project 1967

Medical Academy, Ulm. Project I 1965

58

Conference Center Roof, Riyadh. Project 1966

Sports Center Roofs, Kuwait. Project 1969 (Soap-film and presentation models)

60

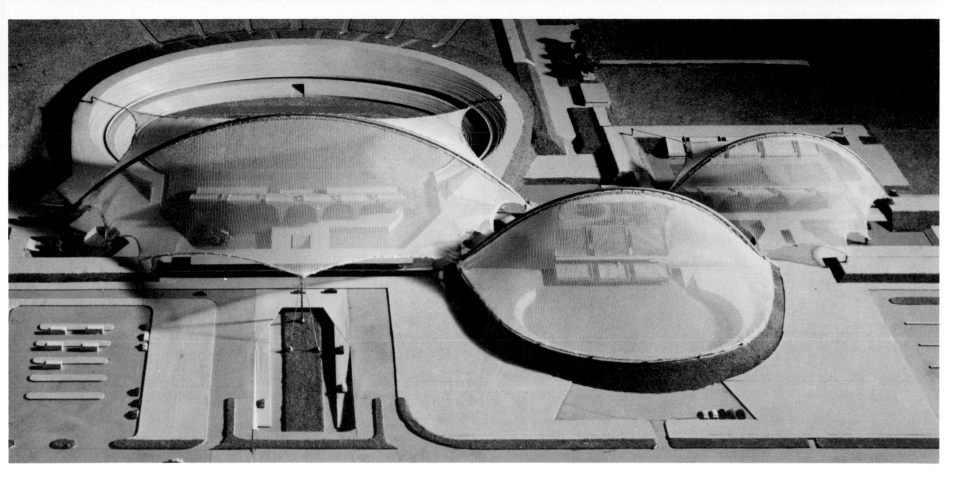

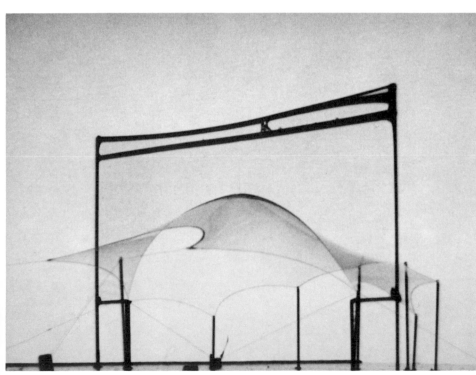

Olympic Stadium Roof, Berlin. Project 1970

Olympic Stadia Roofs, Munich. 1972

Olympic Stadium Roof, Munich. 1972 (Study and stress test models)

64

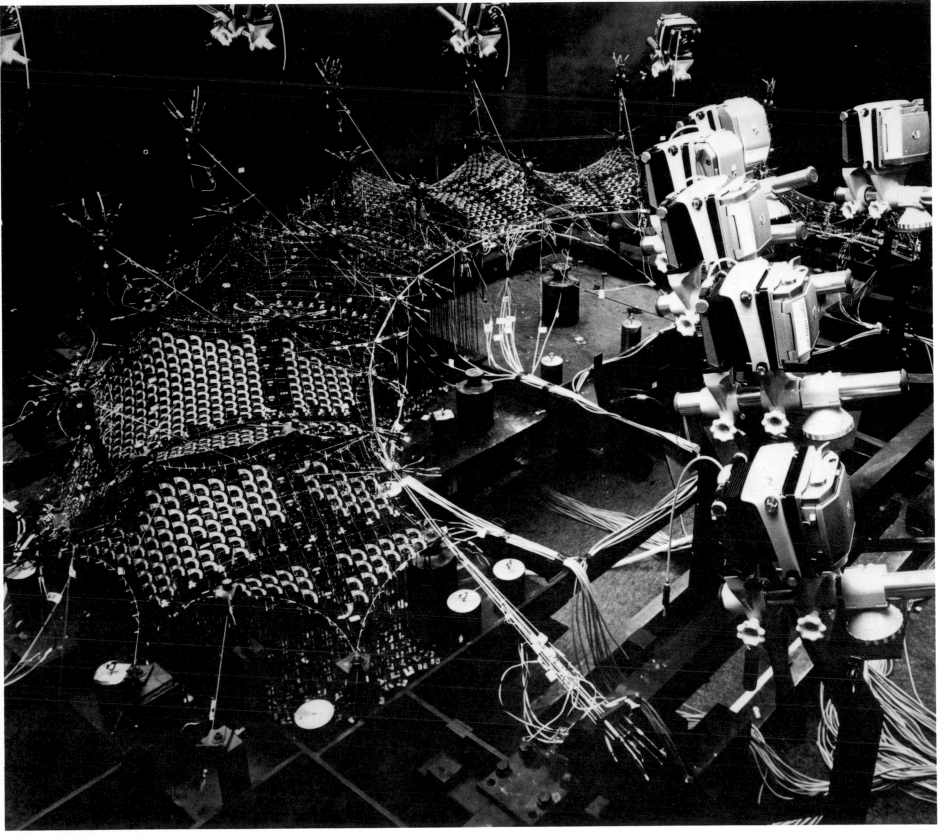

Retractable Roofs

While working on large-scale tensile structures, Frei Otto developed a specialized application—the retractable roof. Like sails, the membranes can be moved along their supporting cables by means of pulleys and winches, or by electric cable tractors expressly developed for these roofs. The first, modest and manually operated, retractable tent was installed in 1965 over a theater terrace at the Casino in Cannes. Larger roofs that can be furled and unfurled automatically in minutes followed for the Open-Air Theater in Bad Hersfeld, and for swimming pools in Paris and Lyons. For such sports facilities, retractable roofs have the particular advantage of extending their utilization through all seasons. The latest design in this series is a mass-production prototype for an automated umbrella structure that is adaptable to smaller and more irregular sites. The retractable roofs approach Frei Otto's ideal of "non-structures" since they impose, in a retracted state, minimum restrictions on their environment. But even fully unfurled, their lightness and translucency seem to provide a more congenial enclosure for activities underneath than most conventional roofs.

Open-Air Theater Roof, Nijmegen. Project 1960

Terrace Roof, Cannes. 1965

Swimming Pool Roof, Lyons. 1970

70

Following pages: Open-Air Theater Roof, Bad Hersfeld. 1968

71

Open-Air Theater Roof, Bad Hersfeld. 1968

74

Ice-Skating Rink Roof, Conflans-Ste. Honorine. Project 1969

Automatic Umbrella Roofs, Cologne. 1971

76

Experimental Studies

These experimental studies, which Frei Otto undertook between 1961 and 1963, represent research projects at the periphery of his primary field. He again investigated suspension structures, which had been the subject of his thesis on hanging roofs. Although they still fall in the category of tensile structures, they are, in most cases, load-stabilized rather than prestressed—the principle of most suspension bridges that are stabilized by the weight of the road deck. With the moveable vertebrae column he devised a structural system that incorporates equal amounts of compression and tension forces. In other examples, like the lattice domes, he produced a pure compression structure by literally inverting a tensile configuration. The result was a new method of vault construction through deformation of a plane lattice grid, which was first used for the auditorium of the German Pavilion in Montreal. In applying his minimal theories to support elements and space frames he arrived at lighter structures by reducing the buckling lengths of their compression members. The resulting forms are distinctly organic and indicative of Frei Otto's interest in the structural patterns extant in nature.

Tree Structures. Project 1960

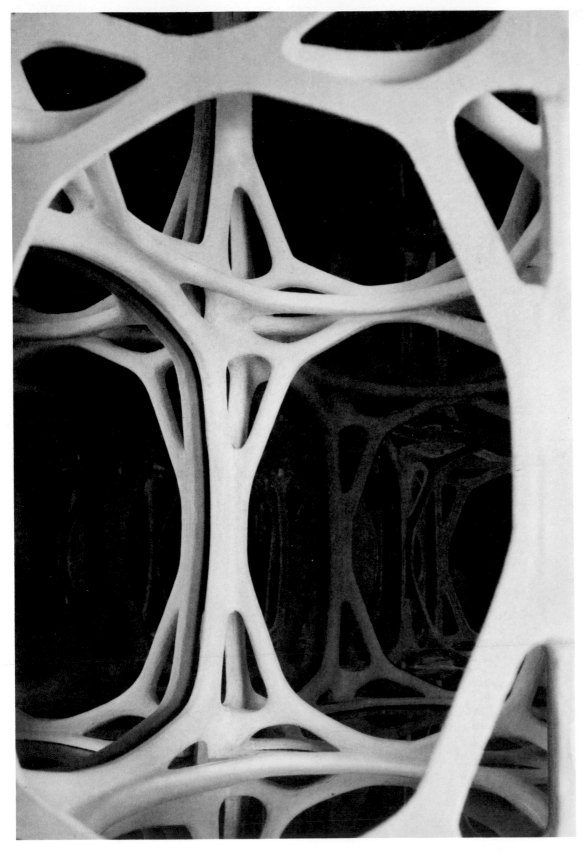

Space Frames. Project 1962

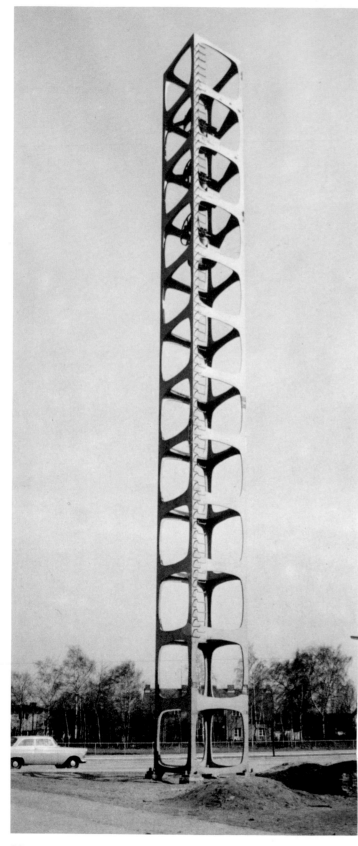

Bell Tower, Berlin-Schönow. 1963

Flexible Column. Project 1963

Medical Academy, Ulm. Project III 1965

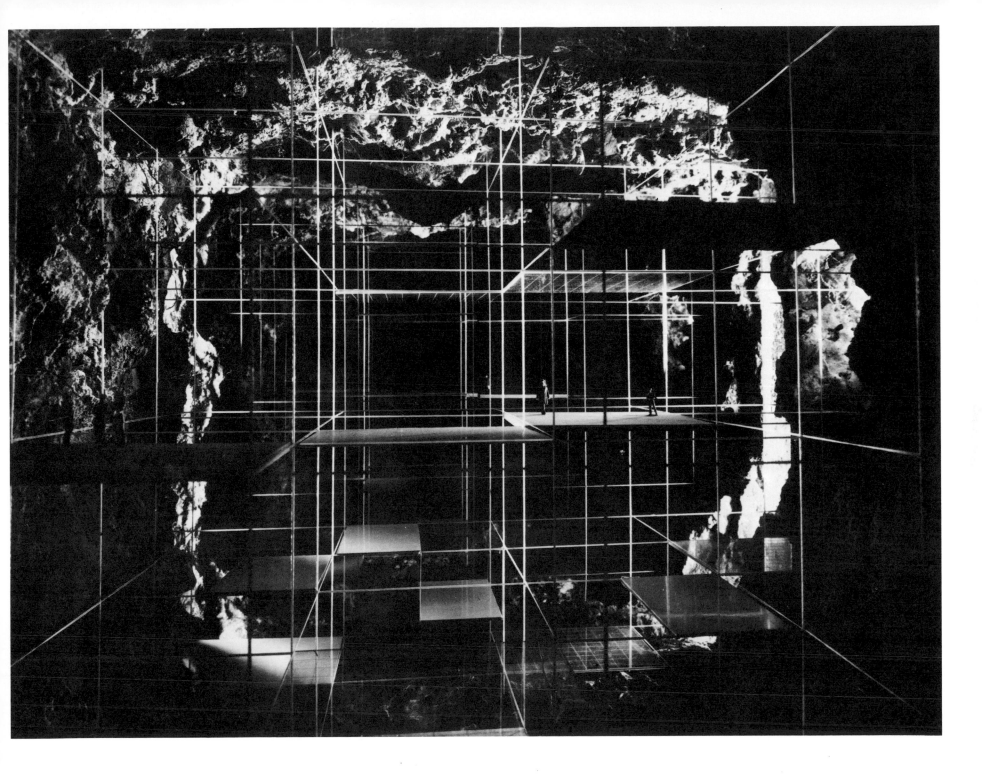

Underground Research Facility. Project 1964

Exhibition Structure, Essen. 1962

Auditorium of German Pavilion, Montreal. 1967

Pneumatic Membranes

Pneumatically distended membranes are minimal structures *par excellence* since they do not require cables and masts but just air pressure to support them. If no imposed loads like snow or wind pressure act upon the membranes they are practically in a state of weightlessness. The new synthetic fabrics make it theoretically possible to span distances of several miles with inflated membranes, and the limitations are less structural than economical, for instance, in terms of energy consumed to maintain the necessary air pressure. Although the number of pneumatic structures executed in the past two decades provided considerable practical experiences, Frei Otto formulated the first coherent theory. From 1959 to 1961 he was almost exclusively occupied with research in the field of inflated membranes, and in 1962 he published the results in the first volume of his work on tensile structures. In the course of his investigations Frei Otto developed a remarkable number of new structural types—either by combining the standard spherical shapes or by varying the shapes and their plan configuration by means of restraining cables and cable nets. In applying his previously gained experiences of tent structures, he was able to reduce and vary the membrane height and provide interior drainage in analogy to the high-and-low-point principle. The theoretical studies were paralleled by the continuous search for practical applications, ranging from hanging grain silos to giant greenhouse envelopes.

Arctic City Envelope. Project 1971

Domed Hall. Project 1959

High-Voltage Test Laboratory,
Cologne, 1966

Missile Installation Cover. Project 1959

Factory Roof. Project 1959
Offshore Storage Facility. Project 1958/1959

Large-Scale Envelope for Agricultural Use. Project 1959

Convention and Exhibition Hall, Chicago. Project 1960

Oil Storage Tanks. Project 1959
Exhibition Hall Roof. Project 1959

Silos for Grain or Cement. Project 1959

Water Tower. Project 1959

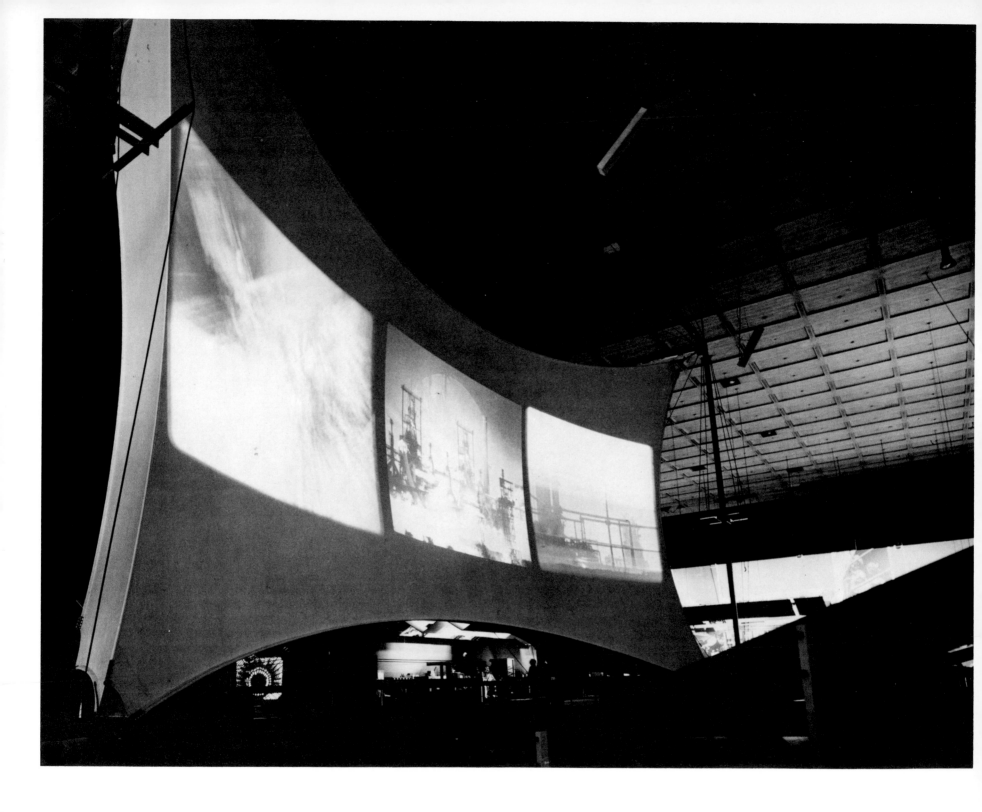

Projection Screen, Berlin. 1968

102

Catalogue

Glossary

Tensile structures are characterized by the prevalence of tension forces in their structural systems and by the limitation of compression forces to a few support members. Thus these lightweight structures do not require the considerable amount of construction materials needed in conventional buildings to absorb the buckling and bending moments in compression members. Membranes are *prestressed* by means of induced forces, which are extant when no other force such as dead weight or an imposed load acts upon the structural systems. *Minimal surfaces* are the smallest possible surfaces between curved linear boundaries (as demonstrated in soap-film tests). *Anticlastic or saddlelike* shapes are produced by curvatures, which intersect at right angles but extend in opposite directions. They ensure the rigidity of cable and mast supported membranes, which are less subject to gravitational than wind forces.

The two main categories of tensile structures are mast and cable supported membranes and pneumatically distended membranes. Examples in the first category are classified according to their supports systems:
1. *Simple saddle membrane* with linear perimeter supports (the primary shape between opposite pairs of support and anchor points, and their variations); 2. *Ridge-type membrane* with linear internal and perimeter supports (additive series of simple saddle shapes between supporting and restraining ridges); 3. *Arch-type membrane* with continuous linear internal support (simple saddle shapes on either side of the supporting arch); 4. *High-point-type membrane* with multiple internal point supports (composite saddle shapes between masts with acute heads or so-called humped surfaces around masts with enlarged heads, each in combination with alternating low-point anchorages).

Supporting or restraining cables are carried directly to the ground at anchor points, and over poles or masts at stabilization points.

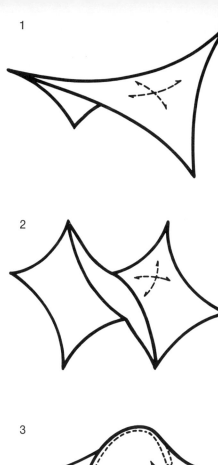

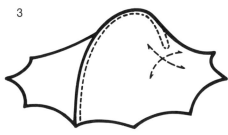

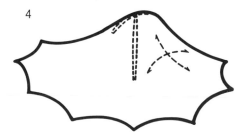

Catalogue

All projects listed on the following pages are prestressed tensile structures unless otherwise indicated. They are shown according to structural categories or practical applications of the various tent types, following the order in which the plates appear. Descriptive data is given to identify primary structural elements and boundary conditions. All measurements are rounded out to full or half units. The architects and engineers with whom Frei Otto collaborated are listed for each project, without any indication of the size or importance of their respective contributions. Page numbers refer to illustrations.

The Bandstand, the first of Frei Otto's executed tensile structures, is the archetype of the prestressed membrane—a square surface stretched by edge wire ropes between opposite high and low points. The resulting curves, identical but reversed, produce the classic saddle-like shape. Like a diagram, it reveals the stresses active in such minimal surfaces, which, in their appearance, combine lightness with strength. The extremely thin membrane—less than 1 millimeter (0.04 inches)—has sufficient rigidity to withstand the strongest winds. The simplicity of the saddle shape allows repetition and arrangement in groups, as was done at the "Interbau" Exhibition two years later.

Bandstand
Federal Garden Exhibition
Kassel, Germany 1955

saddle-type membrane with 2 support points and 2 anchor points

lateral length: 12.50 meters (41 feet), maximum height: 5 meters (17 feet)

translucent cotton canvas, wire ropes, pine-wood poles

(in collaboration with Mattern, Lohs)

page 13

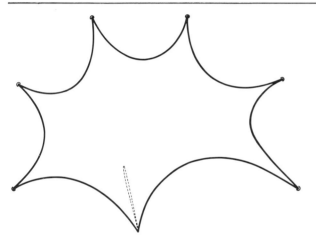

Commissioned to design a temporary shelter at the Rhine riverside for visitors to the Garden Exhibition, Frei Otto introduced a variation of the basic formula — a tilted saddle-type surface with only one high point. The saddle curves appear here vertically and horizontally. Originating in a radial ground plane, the vertical curves converge almost tangentially at the top of the pole. This movement is reinforced by the pattern of the canvas strips which overlap toward the top of the membrane in the area of greatest stress. The inclination of the pole and the curvature of the side ends of the membrane produce a shallow, grotto-like space.

Shelter Pavilion
Federal Garden Exhibition
Cologne, Germany 1957

saddle-type membrane with 1 support point and 6 anchor points

height of pole: 6 meters (20 feet)

colored cotton canvas, edge wire ropes, spindle-shaped pole

(in collaboration with Bubner, Lohs, Frank)

pages 14, 15

Peaked shapes were the thematic requirement for this section of the exhibition, and saddle surfaces supported at one point were the obvious choice as symbols of the Swiss Alps. The large scale of these tents required a wire-rope net as the primary tension structure; the ropes were encased in plastic so that the covering fabric could be sewn onto the net. The edge wire ropes at the base form a diamond shape with long extensions toward the anchor points, where concrete pillars raise the membranes above the ground. This allows an overlapping and more landscape-like arrangement of the pavilions.

Exhibition Pavilions "Neiges et Rocs,"
Harbor Section
Swiss National Exhibition
Lausanne, Switzerland 1964

saddle-type net with 1 support point and 4 anchor points

5 units—maximum span: 36 meters (118 feet), mast length: 24 meters (79 feet)

steel wire-rope net with attached colored canvas, edge wire ropes, lattice steel mast

(in collaboration with Saugey, Hertling, Romberg, Röder)

pages 16–18

Dance Pavilion
Federal Garden Exhibition
Cologne, Germany 1957

radial ridge-type membrane with central tension ring, 6 support points, and 6 anchor points

maximum diameter: 31.50 meters (103 feet), maximum height: 10 meters (33 feet)

coated, translucent cotton canvas, radial and edge wire ropes, 6 lattice steel masts

(in collaboration with Bubner, Lohs, Frank)

pages 19, 20

The roof above this outdoor dance floor is an example of Frei Otto's ability to adapt a structure to a specific site. For this circular platform inside a circular reflecting pool, he devised a radial arrangement of multiple saddle surfaces between low restraining and high supporting ridges, the latter carried by perimeter masts. All of the ridge cables converge from their anchorage points at the pool's outer edge toward a tension ring in the center of the membrane. Although open in all directions, the membrane deflects sound and light onto the dance floor and protects it from rain. The undulating shape alters the roof's appearance at every vantage point, relieving its strict symmetry.

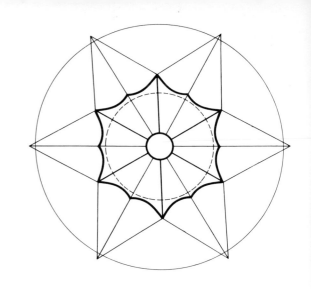

Hangar Tents
Mass-produced by L. Stromeyer and Company
Konstanz, Germany, since 1957

parallel ridge-type membrane with 2 support points and 6 anchor points per unit

tent model "WN 16.2": 3 units—36 x 30 meters (118 x 98 feet), height at center: 8.50 meters (28 feet), total weight: 4,200 kilograms (9,260 pounds)

cotton canvas or synthetic fabrics, connector wire ropes, poles with spring tensioning devices, anchors

(in collaboration with L. Stromeyer and Company)

pages 21, 22

The manufacturer who produced and erected most of Frei Otto's tensile structures asked him to develop several types of tents for mass production. The commission for the small aircraft hangars in 1954 led to an investigation of prestressed saddle surfaces between ridges. These are formed by parallel cables, alternately supporting the membrane between poles or restraining it between anchor points. While such undulating surfaces consume more material and increase the number of anchor points, they reduce the tension force required at each individual anchorage. This is a decisive advantage for tents, which, despite their size, still have to be erected with conventional means.

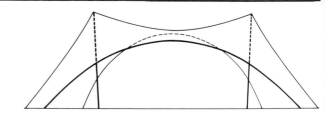

Wave Hall
International Horticultural Exhibition
Hamburg, Germany 1963

main hall—parallel ridge-type membrane of 6 bays with a total of 6 support and 7 restraining ridges and 26 anchor points

passage gallery—parallel ridge-type membrane of 11 bays (6 part of main hall) with a total of 17 stabilization points and 21 anchor points

main hall—length: 82 meters (269 feet), width of bay: 12.50 meters (41 feet), span between masts: 20 meters (66 feet), height at center: 5.20 meters (17 feet)

coated cotton canvas, transverse and edge wire ropes, steel lattice masts, guyed poles

(in collaboration with Habermann, Hertling, Koch)

pages 23–25

Wave Hall is the most sculptural and complex of the undulating tents. It is not only asymmetrical in section but also comprises two structurally different elements. The hall itself employs saddle surfaces between parallel ridges that, alternately, support or restrain the membrane. The masts under the supporting ridges are higher on one side than on the other, causing the asymmetrical deflection of the ridge contours. The second element, a passage gallery, which for half of its length is directly connected to the main membrane, represents a row of simple saddle surfaces. Made of canvas strips 1 meter (3 feet) wide, the membrane clearly reveals its tension pattern when the interior is lit at night.

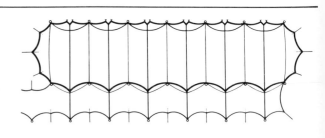

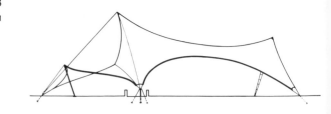

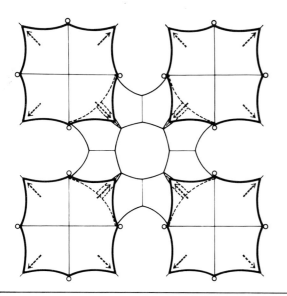

The four pavilions adjoining Wave Hall utilize the same ridge principle in a different, but equally imaginative, way. Their saddle surfaces are formed between two supporting, and two restraining, ridges which alternately cross each other at 45 degree angles. All surfaces are symmetrically delineated by identical edge curves on all sides. The supporting ridges produce acute, almost vertical, corners, which emphasize the steep mast peaks. Raised above the ground, the four square tents overlap a central connecting gallery. Its simple saddle surfaces are connected to a central tension ring and carried around the masts under the pavilions.

Small Pavilions
International Horticultural Exhibition
Hamburg, Germany 1963

main pavilions—radial ridge-type membrane with 4 support and 4 restraining ridges and 8 anchor points

central connecting passage—radial saddle-type membrane with central tension ring, 12 support points, and 8 anchor points

main pavilions (4 units)—lateral length: 15 meters (49 feet), maximum height: 8 meters (26 feet), diagonal span between masts: 18 meters (59 feet)

coated cotton canvas, radial and edge wire ropes, steel lattice masts

(in collaboration with Habermann, Hertling, Koch)
pages 26–28

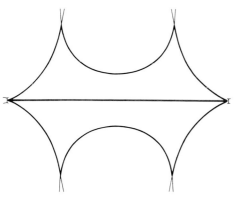

Arch-supported prestressed membranes combine the advantages of two systems, and are able to span large areas. While the arch provides continuous support for the membrane, the saddle surfaces stabilize the arch laterally and permit considerable reduction of its volume. The membrane is the first produced from a fabric made of glass filaments. More durable but less expansible than canvas, it has to be assembled with utmost precision to conform with the established curvatures. Although it has a simple symmetrical configuration, the Entrance Arch provides a wide diversity of views.

Entrance Arch
Federal Garden Exhibition
Cologne, Germany 1957

arch-supported, saddle-type membrane with 4 stabilization points

maximum span: 34 meters (112 feet), maximum height: 6 meters (20 feet), arch tube diameter: 19 centimeters (7½ inches)

coated glass-fiber fabric, edge wire ropes, tubular steel arch, 4 guyed poles

(in collaboration with Bubner, Lohs, Frank)
page 29

Initially conceived with a supporting arch, the roof was designed and executed eight years later as a suspended membrane. A row of high points in the saddle surface provide the connection with the cables extending from two lateral masts. The membrane itself retained the original shape determined to a great degree by the site; since a picturesque mountain forms the backdrop for the open stage, the rows of seating had to be cantilevered above the slope. The nearly identical views of the model and the completed roof reflect the fundamental role of models in the design of tension structures.

Open-Air Theater
Wunsiedel, Germany 1962–1970

saddle-type membrane with 5 suspension points, 6 stabilization points, and 8 anchor points

covered area: 1,000 square meters (1,200 square yards), mast height: 21 meters (69 feet)

translucent synthetic fabric, edge and suspension wire ropes, 2 lattice steel masts

(in collaboration with Habermann, Koch, Minke, Romberg)
pages 30, 31

Humped Pavilion
Federal Garden Exhibition
Cologne, Germany 1957

high-point-type membrane with 2 support points
and 9 anchor points

maximum length: 24 meters (79 feet), height of
poles: 4 meters (14 feet)

yellow cotton canvas, edge wire ropes, and poles
with heads of capped spreader bars

(in collaboration with Bubner, Lohs, Frank)

pages 32, 33

The Humped Pavilion, the second of Frei Otto's
shelter tents at the Garden Exhibition, was an important prototype. The two symmetrical halves of the
membrane each have one high point, and intersecting saddle surfaces. Unlike the high points in other
tensile structures, these have rounded hump-like
shapes. Devices attached to the tops of the poles
provide an enlarged resilient surface which facili-
tates load transmission and erection procedure. The
membrane can be tied down first and then pushed
up by means of the poles. While the Humped Pavilion
was shaped after an elaborate pattern, later and
larger membranes have been made of parallel strips
of canvas.

Interbau Café
"Interbau" International Building Exhibition
Berlin, Germany 1957

high-point-type membrane with 8 offset support
points, 3 restraining ridges, and 14 anchor points

length 28 meters (92 feet), width: 24 meters (79 feet),
axial compression (transmitted at each support
point): 850 kilograms (1,873 pounds)

synthetic fabric, edge cables, telescopic poles of
varying heights with star-shaped heads of resilient
plywood blades

(in collaboration with Bubner, Lohs, Frank)

page 34

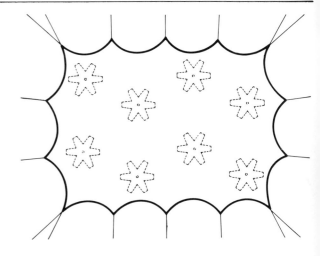

Exhibition Hall "The City of Tomorrow"
"Interbau" International Building Exhibition
Berlin, Germany 1957

high-point-type membrane continuously attached
to a space frame at bay intervals and raised at
8 points in each of the 10 bays

length: 100 meters (328 feet), width: 52 meters
(171 feet), length of support blades: 3 meters
(10 feet)

coated translucent cotton canvas, steel struts with
spring tensioning devices and resilient
pine-wood blades

(in collaboration with Karl Otto, Günschel)

page 35

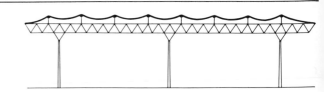

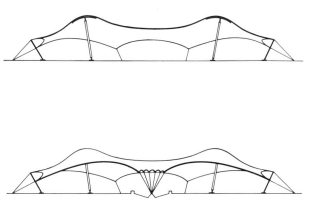

This high-and-low-point membrane has proven most efficient in covering large surfaces. Made of straight fabric bands, the membrane requires no pattern cuts. Its shape is the result of deflection at the high and low points. The humps are produced by the mastheads, which transmit a prestressing force onto the membrane. The three low points in the center axis are tied to the ground by a parachute-like cable arrangement. Their circular openings allow drainage to basins below. The cable-reinforced edge of the membrane is secured by guyed masts or, at alternating points, anchored directly to the ground. Contributing to the roof's economy is its short erection time: it took 17 men only 15 hours.

Membrane Hall
International Horticultural Exhibition
Hamburg, Germany 1963

high-and-low-point membrane with 8 support points, 3 central and 26 peripheral anchor points

length: 64 meters (210 feet), width: 29 meters (95 feet), maximum height: 5.50 meters (18 feet)

heavy translucent cotton, edge cables, steel masts with plywood-blade heads

(in collaboration with Habermann, Hertling, Koch)

pages 36, 37

Frei Otto and Rolf Gutbrod attempted, with this competition-winning project, to create a man-made landscape. The cavernous interior contained modular steel platforms arranged at different levels. The entire area was covered by a single membrane of irregular plan and varying heights. Its contours were determined by the high points of the masts and the low points where the membrane was drawn, funnel-like, down to the ground. Eye loops filled with clear plastic material accentuated these points and the saddle surfaces they created. The prestressed membrane consisted of a translucent skin hung from a steel wire net, which, by eye, ridge, and edge ropes, was connected with the mast heads and anchor blocks.

Pavilion of the Federal Republic of Germany
World Exposition
Montreal, Canada 1967

composite high-and-low-point net with 8 support points, 3 restraining points in combination with 3 continuous ridges, 31 perimeter anchor points

maximum length: 130 meters (427 feet), maximum width: 105 meters (345 feet), covered area: 8,000 square meters (86,000 square feet), mast heights: 14 to 38 meters (46 to 125 feet)

net wire ropes; edge, eye, and ridge wire ropes; turnbuckle hangers; hung translucent synthetic fabric, tapered tubular steel masts

(in collaboration with Gutbrod, Kiess, Kendel, Medlin)

pages 39–53

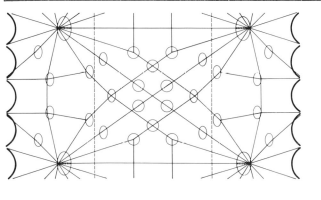

The dock cover is one of the largest and most daring schemes that Frei Otto has developed in detail. While the feasibility of such structures had been generally accepted, their economic advantages were established for the first time in this project. The enormous roof would accelerate the loading and unloading operations by protecting them from adverse weather. A parallel row of masts on either side of the dock carries a primary cable network, which in turn supports a wire net membrane. The surface of the membrane has a low curvature offering minimum wind resistance. The high-point deflections serve as connecting elements for the supporting cable network.

Dock Cover
Weser River Port Extension
Bremen, Germany
Project 1961

high-point-type net with 4 primary and 28 secondary suspension points and 8 anchor points per bay

8 bays—length: 1,500 meters (4,930 feet), span: 380 meters (1,250 feet), quayside height: 52.50 meters (172 feet), covered area: 500,000 square meters (124 acres), mast length: 85 meters (279 feet), width of bay: 170 meters (558 feet)

primary (suspension) network wire ropes, secondary (enclosure) network wire ropes with square mesh and attached sheet-metal panels, guyed steel masts

(in collaboration with Budde, Heinrich, Schröck)

pages 54, 55

Construction Site Cover
North Peckham Redevelopment
Borough of Southwark, England
Project 1965

high-point-type membrane with 25 suspension points and 9 stabilization points

36 demountable units—lateral length between masts: 30 meters (100 feet), mean height: 20 meters (65 feet)

coated synthetic fabric, suspension and stabilization wire ropes, 3-part tubular steel masts

(in collaboration with Romberg, Röder, Lehmbrock)

page 56

Attempts to protect construction sites from the cost-increasing effects of adverse weather have been made for some time. The first systematic solution was prepared by Frei Otto for the London Borough of Southwark to shelter the North Peckham Housing Project. As construction of all of the six-story houses would not have started simultaneously on the 160,000 square meter (40 acre) site, a demountable system was developed comprising 36 modular units. Their components are adjustable guyed masts, a primary supporting net, and membrane roof and wall elements. Standardization of the components would allow mass production and economical use for most conventional building sites.

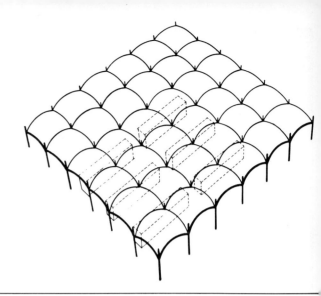

Indian Pavilion for World Exposition
Osaka, Japan
Project 1967

radial space net with 5 primary support points and 10 perimeter anchor points

maximum diameter: 15 meters (49 feet), height: 27 meters (89 feet), space-net mesh: 50 centimeters (20 inches) in each dimension

wire ropes, coated canvas, steel mast with 5 cantilevered struts

(in collaboration with Patel/National Design Institute, Ahmedabad)

page 57

The program adopted for the Indian Pavilion at Osaka called less for the display of artefacts than for continuous performances and participatory events. In addition, economic considerations demanded that the Pavilion be demountable for further use. Its primary structure consists of a mast with five booms cantilevered from its top, and supporting wire ropes carried over the booms from the mast head to their radial anchor points. These wire ropes supported the saddle-shaped membrane sections as well as the radial space net, which filled the interior and was meant to receive standardized platforms at various levels for different activities.

Medical Academy
Ulm, Germany
Project (Version I) 1965

radial net with one main support point and continuous anchorage ring on 58 inverted V-supports

3 units—maximum diameter: 56 meters (184 feet), maximum height: 20 meters (66 feet)

bent steel T-beams and circumferential wire ropes, glass infill, tubular steel mast with ring crown

(in collaboration with Romberg, Scherzinger, Röder)

page 58

For the Medical Academy Frei Otto submitted three different proposals, each giving equal consideration to internal flexibility. The first version envisaged three large interconnected glass cones covering 8,500 square meters (91,500 square feet) of modular building units underneath. From a supporting column in the center, steel T-beams would be hung radially and braced by circumferential cables. Bent inward by their weight, the beams would be connected at the bottom to an edge ring resting on inverted V-shaped supports. As the entire surface between the beams would have been filled in with glass panels, the interior had to be protected from glare by cotton sails.

Hotel and Conference Center
Riyadh, Saudi Arabia
Competition Project 1966

polygonal net combined with radial net (as part of the central support system), 14 anchor points and 14 stabilization points

maximum height: 47 meters (154 feet), maximum length: 196 meters (643 feet)

steel cables, white aluminum sheeting (polygonal net) and adjustable louvers (radial net), tubular steel mast with conical support head serving as water-tower reservoir

(in collaboration with Gutbrod, Kendel, Arup & Partners)

page 59

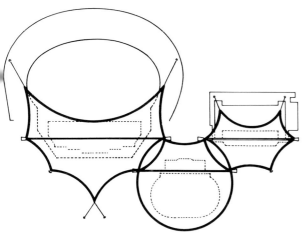

The project with which Kenzo Tange and Frei Otto won the competition for the 1974 Pan-Arabic Olympic Games complex in Kuwait was primarily dictated by climatic considerations. The stadia are at least partially roofed and closely aligned on either side of a sunken and covered pedestrian mall. For all three, Frei Otto designed similar arch-supported membranes varying in plan and arch radius. Made of wire rope nets, the roofs of the main stadium and the swimming pool will be covered with aluminum mesh, while the indoor arena will be closed with aluminum sheeting. The minimal surfaces of these large membranes were established by means of soap-film models.

Roofs for Sports Center Stadia
Kuwait, Kuwait
Competition Project 1969

arch-supported saddle-type nets with 7, 4, and 6 anchor points

main stadium—arch span: 240 meters (787 feet), covered area: 23,000 square meters (248,000 square feet)
indoor arena—arch span: 150 meters (492 feet), covered area: 14,500 square meters (156,000 square feet)
swimming pool—arch span: 120 meters (394 feet), covered area: 7,000 square meters (76,000 square feet)
maximum diameter of arch pipe: 1.50 meters (5 feet)

wire rope nets with attached aluminum mesh (main stadium, swimming pool), aluminum sheet (indoor arena), edge wire ropes, tubular steel arches

(in collaboration with Tange, URTEC)

pages 60, 61

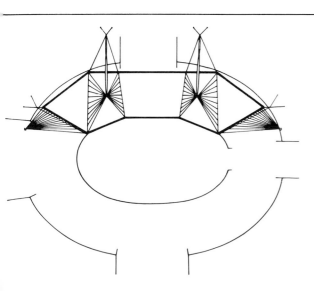

Roof for Olympic Stadium
Berlin, Germany
Competition Project 1970

suspension roof stabilized by weight of construction (one-directional net of cables and transverse beams) with 4 transverse lines of suspension and 6 anchor points

maximum length: 250 meters (820 feet), maximum width: 72 meters (236 feet), covered area: 13,140 square meters (142,000 square feet), maximum height of roof: 40 meters (131 feet)

net and suspension wire ropes, reinforced concrete beams, transparent acrylic sheets, lattice steel masts

(in collaboration with Gutbrod, Arup & Partners, Happold, Oleiko, Rice, Thorsteinn)

page 62

Roof for Olympic Stadium
Munich, Germany 1972

saddle-type nets (9 units) with 2 suspension points, 2 understayed support points, 4 anchor points per unit, and 1 continuous frontal edge cable for all units

maximum span: 65 meters (213 feet), length of edge cable: 440 meters (1,443 feet), maximum height: 58 meters (190 feet), roof area: 34,000 square meters (366,000 square feet)

net wire ropes, translucent acrylic sheeting, tubular steel masts

(in collaboration with Behnisch & Partner, Bubner, Leonhardt, Andrä)

pages 63–65

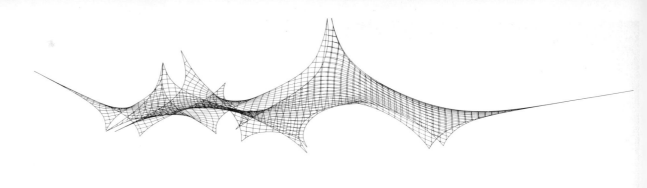

Roof configuration above entrance area, drawn by a computer

Roof for Olympic Athletic Arena
Munich, Germany 1972

saddle-type net (5 main units and 8 eye units) with 2 suspension points, 2 central understayed support points, 8 support points, and 29 anchor points

maximum span: 135 meters (443 feet), maximum height: 55 meters (180 feet), roof area: 22,000 square meters (237,000 square feet)

net wire ropes, translucent acrylic sheeting, tubular steel masts

(in collaboration with Behnisch & Partner, Bubner, Leonhardt, Andrä)

page 63

The architects of the stadia and supporting facilities for the Olympic Games at Munich attempted to create one environmental entity. According to their concept, Frei Otto developed tent shapes which adhere to the same structural formula and appear as units of one long roof. Like an extended arc, they cover half of the main stadium at one end, the athletic and swimming arenas at the other end, and the main entrance area in the center. Saddle-shaped wire rope nets, suspended from masts and anchored to the ground, constitute the primary structure, which supports the protecting membrane of clear plastic sheeting.

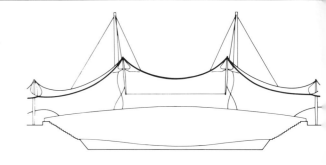

Roof for Olympic Swimming Arena
Munich, Germany 1972

saddle-type membrane with 1 suspension point and 13 stabilization and anchor points

maximum span: 85 meters (279 feet), maximum height: 50 meters (164 feet), roof area: 12,000 square meters (130,000 square feet)

wire ropes, coated synthetic fabric, tubular steel mast

(in collaboration with Behnisch & Partner, Bubner, Leonhardt, Andrä)

page 63

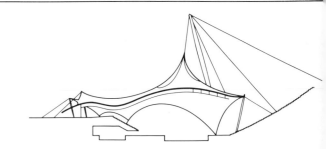

Roof for Open-Air Theater
Nijmegen, The Netherlands
Project 1960

retractable saddle-type membranes, 3 main units, each suspended from one mast and radial cable sets, 2 intermediate units suspended from auxiliary masts, one frontal edge cable for all units

maximum span: 68 meters (223 feet), mast heights: 12–16 meters (39–53 feet), covered area: 1,200 square meters (12,900 square feet)

translucent synthetic fabric, manual and automatic retracting devices, wire ropes, steel masts

(in collaboration with Wehrhahn)

page 67

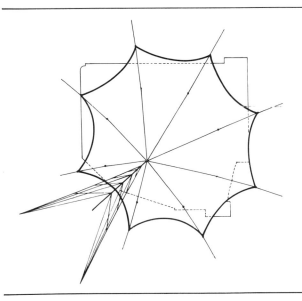

For his first retractable roof, Frei Otto adapted an earlier research project since the structure had to be designed, produced, and erected within three and a half months. The existing terrace and adjoining building cause the membrane's inclination toward the ground plane and its eccentric suspension point. The peak-furled membrane, composed of saddle-shaped segments, has the appearance of an octagonal pyramid. At the edge and high points, the membrane is attached to pulleys which move on the radial supporting cables between the mast head and anchor points. Assembled from thin steel pipes in an inverted parabolic curve, the mast is guyed by two sets of cables.

Roof for Terrace
Palm Beach Casino
Cannes, France 1965

retractable, radial saddle-type membrane suspended from guyed mast and, at 16 points, from cable tractors on 8 stationary cables

maximum span: 34.50 meters (113 feet), maximum height: 15 meters (49 feet)

coated synthetic fabric, cable pulleys, wire ropes, curved wire-supported mast

(in collaboration with Taillibert, Romberg, Scherzinger, Edzard, Gentsch)

pages 68, 69

Retractable-membrane roofs have an obvious advantage for open swimming pools, extending their use throughout all seasons. Since the interior is heated with warm air, snow melts on the membrane surface and poses no load problem. This executed roof follows the scheme of Bad Hersfeld: radial cables, extending from the top of one mast carry the cable tractors and the attached membrane, which, to counter wind forces, has a slightly spherical shape. Retractable roofs are not only more economical than comparable clear-span structures, their lightness and translucency seem also more appropriate for a swimming pool.

Roof for Swimming Pool
Intercommunal Pool, St. Fons
Lyons, France 1970

retractable high-point-type membrane suspended at 14 peripheral and 16 internal points from cable tractors on stationary wire ropes extending radially from one supporting mast

length: 62 meters (203 feet), width: 33 meters (108 feet), maximum height: 9.50 meters (31 feet), mast height: 30.50 meters (100 feet)

translucent synthetic fabric, electric cable tractors, automatic steering device, wire ropes, steel mast

(in collaboration with Taillibert, du Chateau, Romberg, Röder)

pages 70, 71

Roof for Open-Air Theater
Abbey Ruin
Bad Hersfeld, Germany 1968

retractable high-point-type membrane suspended at 14 peripheral and 7 internal points from cable tractors on 14 stationary wire ropes extending radially from one supporting mast to 5 stabilization points

length: 46 meters (151 feet), width: 31 meters (102 feet), maximum height: 16 meters (53 feet), average retraction speed: 4 minutes

coated heavy synthetic fabric, electric cable tractors and automatic steering device, wire ropes, steel masts

(in collaboration with Romberg, Röder, Krier)

pages 72–74

The Abbey Ruin has for decades been the scene of major summer theater festivals. The problem was not only to protect the audience from sudden rain but to do so in a way that would not interfere with the important remains of Romanesque architecture. The solution Frei Otto proposed was a retractable membrane roof that could be automatically unfurled at great speed. It required one high mast placed outside the nave to support the radical cables and the retracted membrane. Suspended at its perimeter points as well as internal high points, the membrane is unfurled by cable tractors, which, powered by an electric motor, crawl along the cables.

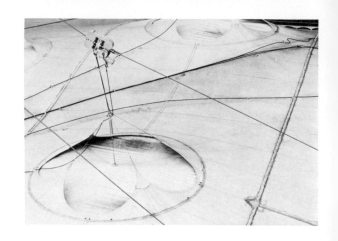

Roof for Ice-Skating Rink
Conflans-Ste. Honorine, France
Project 1969

retractable high-point-type membrane suspended at 14 internal and 32 peripheral points from cable tractors moving on 10 radial arches

length: 80 meters (262 feet), width: 50 meters (164 feet), maximum height: 15 meters (49 feet)

coated synthetic fabric, electric cable tractors and automatic steering device, steel arches, transverse wire ropes

(in collaboration with Blasko, Bubner, Oleiko, Krier)

page 75

In this project for a retractable roof over an ice-skating rink, mast and cables are substituted by a series of arches. They extend radially from the center of one side over the oblong rink surface and are braced by circumferential cables. The cable tractors move here in tracks on the underside of the arches when furling or unfurling the membrane. As the membrane also has to enclose the space from the sides, its shape is more curved toward the perimeter and shows a slight depression in the center.

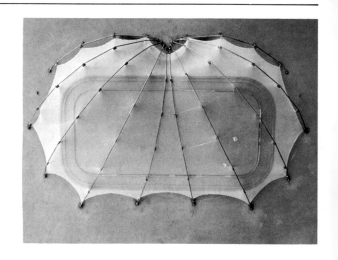

Automatic Umbrella Roofs
Federal Garden Exhibition
Cologne, Germany 1971

retractable, radial saddle-type membrane with 9 support points (at ends of collapsible spokes) and anchorage base (around umbrella pole)

8 units—diameter: 16 meters (53 feet), height at edge: 5.5–9.5 meters (18–31 feet)

coated, translucent synthetic fabric with edge wire ropes; steel pole with automatic spoke mechanism and auxiliary umbrella blades for protection of electric motor and retracted membrane

(in collaboration with Linhardt, Rasch)

pages 76, 77

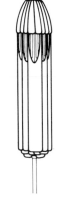 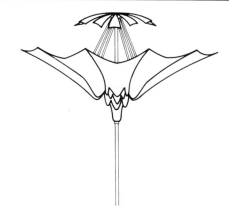 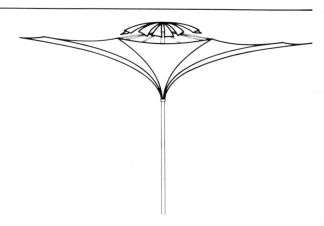

His preoccupation with minimal surfaces led Frei Otto to theoretical observations on the shortest distances between a number of points in space. In this project, undertaken with Yale students, a thin slab was to be supported at a great number of points, and the resulting multiplication of compression members was to be utilized for a reduction of the individual buckling lengths. This, in turn, would yield a reduction in thickness and therefore in material, which serves in compression members mostly to obviate bending. After stiffening the interconnected strands, the model was turned upside down revealing an organic configuration.

Tree Structures
Research Project (Yale University) 1960

ramified compression structure of components with reduced buckling lengths (minimizing the bending moments in the supported plate)

(in collaboration with School of Architecture)

page 79

In extending his theories about minimum surfaces to compression structures, Frei Otto concerned himself with space frames. One way of reducing the required amounts of material is to shorten the buckling length of individual compression members and to arrange them in a pattern which coincides with the shortest path of force transmission without weakening the flexure stiffness of the individual joints. In one case, where all sides of the modular cube have been cut open, rounded corners introduce stiffening flanges in each direction. The other example shows a more dissolved network of bars which circumscribe a dodecagonal opening in the cube surface.

Space Frame Structures
Research Project 1962

space frame structures with flexure-stiff joints, cube as modular component

(in collaboration with Koch, Minke)

pages 80, 81

The Bell Tower is the only executed structure in which Frei Otto's space frame studies have found direct application. Confirmed by computer calculations, the proposed steel lattice frame with flexure-stiff joints provides a most efficient solution. The design of a bell tower has not only to take into account the weight attached to its top but also the considerable oscillation generated by the swinging bells. With a minimum of material and labor, the tower was assembled from steel plates in which slightly rounded openings had been cut automatically by a template-guided profiling machine. Welded together at the factory, the entire tower was transported to the site and erected in four hours.

Bell Tower for Protestant Church
Berlin-Schönow, Germany 1963

space frame structure with rigid joints of 12 units in linear assembly

height: 24 meters (79 feet), lateral length: 2 meters (6½ feet), maximum deflection caused by oscillation: 17 millimeters (11/16 inch)

steel plates automatically cut and factory welded

(in collaboration with Bubner)

page 82

Flexible Column
Research Project 1963

vertebrae-type column with flexible core under compression and cable sets under tension threaded through 3-armed discs with extending and contracting device at bottom to effect desired movements

(in collaboration with Development Center for Lightweight Construction, Berlin)

page 83

Membrane-supporting poles or masts not only consume disproportionate amounts of material but their traditional shapes are also formally incompatible with most tensile structures. In the course of developing different types of latticed or guyed masts, Frei Otto invented the moveable column. It consists of a flexible core, triangular discs decreasing in size toward the top of the column, and wires threaded through holes in the disc arms each terminating at an individual disc. By shortening or lengthening the wire sets from a control device at the base, the column can be turned and bent quickly in any direction.

Medical Academy
Ulm, Germany
Project (Version III) 1965

space net, triangular in section, suspended from a primary cable between supporting internal masts

length: 355 meters (1,165 feet), width (at ground-floor level): 82 meters (269 feet), height: 55 meters (180 feet)

wire ropes, steel masts

(in collaboration with Romberg, Scherzinger, Redlich, Röder, Nedeljkov)

page 84

In the third version of this research hospital, Frei Otto proposed a suspension building as a linear structure. Its shape is determined by the catenary curves of the lateral wire ropes, which anchor the building on either side and support the floor levels inside. These cables are suspended from a primary wire rope, which is carried over the nine masts. The slanted surfaces permit a terraced arrangement of the patients' rooms, leaving the interior for the operating and research facilities. As this project suggests, suspension structures offer possibilities for new building forms, which no longer depend on the traditional post and beam formula.

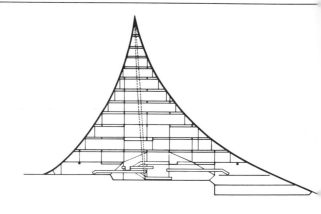

Underground Research Facility
Research Project 1964

suspended space net with horizontally interposed rigid compression members

(in collaboration with Zamboni)

page 85

In the few existing multistory suspension buildings, the horizontal floor levels are supported at the perimeter by wire ropes which are suspended from the top of a solid core containing elevators and utilities. This study exploits the specific site condition of a cave to present a suspension building as a pure tension structure. The space net is absolutely rigid because it can be attached to all sides of the cave. The floor plates, the only compression members, are interposed at random places in the space net. The model produces the contradictory image of the perspective grid which implies infinity of space, subjected to the ultimate confinement of the cave.

The experiences with wire rope net membranes found an experimental application in these compression structures. Their domed shape was achieved by deformation of a plane grid assembled from flexible laths or metal bars. By leaving their joints loose, the laths or bars can move while the grid is lifted up at its center and tied down at its perimeter. The accuracy of the shape depends on precision in predetermining the length of each individual member and the configuration of the grid's base. For this purpose, suspension models are used to reproduce the lattice grid upside down as a hanging net of chains with measurable catenary curves.

Exhibition Structure
German Building Exhibition
Essen, Germany 1962

domed shell structure produced by deformation of a plane lattice grid, bendable members with loose joints tightened for final stabilization, perimeter foundation on a square plan with rounded corners

span: 15 meters (49 feet), maximum height: 5 meters (16 feet)

pine-wood laths, metal bolts

(in collaboration with Koch, Pietsch, Romberg)

page 86

Although compression structures, the lattice domes and vaults have one practical advantage in common with Frei Otto's tension structures: they can be prefabricated and, at least for moderate spans, preassembled at the factory. The flexible joints permit the lattice grids to be collapsed diagonally, facilitating transportation. The roofs for the German Pavilion's 250-seat auditorium and its foyer were designed as lattice domes spanning irregular polygonal spaces. They were attached to the enclosing walls and one common edge beam, and were covered with different insulating materials. Additional loads did not need to be considered as the domes were located inside the Pavilion.

Auditorium of German Pavilion
World Exposition
Montreal, Canada 1967

domed shell structures produced by deformation of a plane lattice grid, bendable members with loose joints tightened for final stabilization, attached to polygonal perimeter walls

auditorium—spans: 17 meters (56 feet) to 13 meters (43 feet)

foyer—spans: 20 meters (66 feet) to 4.5 meters (15 feet)

maximum lath length: 19 meters (62 feet), lattice mesh: 50 centimeters (20 inches)

hemlock-wood laths, metal bolts, wood-cement acoustic panels, plywood sheeting, cotton canvas covering

(in collaboration with Gutbrod, Kiess, Kendel, Medlin)

page 87

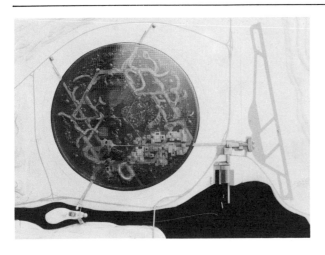

Pneumatically distended membranes are capable of spanning larger areas than any other structure. Commissioned to design a roofed city for a maximum of 45,000 inhabitants in the Arctic, Frei Otto and his team proposed, for the enclosure, a low spherical membrane. Consisting of a transparent synthetic fabric reinforced by an orthogonal net of polyester ropes, the giant envelope would be sustained through internal pressure generated by the city's nuclear-powered air conditioning system. Equipped with moveable lighting as well as shading devices to compensate for the polar extremes of winter and summer the membrane would moderate the climatic conditions to permit vegetation.

Arctic City Envelope
Project 1971

spherical pneumatic membrane with reinforcing rope net

diameter: 2 kilometers (1.24 miles), maximum height: 240 meters (787 feet)

transparent synthetic fabric in 2 layers, high-strength polyester ropes

(in collaboration with Tange, URTEC, Arup & Partners)

page 89

**Domed Hall
Research Project 1959**

composite spherical membranes (to be rigidified after inflation with stiffening compounds to produce a self-supporting shell structure)

(in collaboration with Development Center for Lightweight Construction, Berlin)

page 90

The nature of pneumatically distended membranes, where equal tension is exerted at every point of the surface, favors spherical or cylindrical shapes. One objective of Frei Otto's extensive research was to overcome these formal restrictions through the combination of various shapes which would allow more differentiated spaces. The hall on a mountain top is such a combination, which includes two domes, almost half spheres, and one vertical cylinder with a spherical top.

**High-Voltage Test Laboratory
Felten & Guilleaume Company
Cologne, Germany 1966**

spherical pneumatic membrane with restraining cable between intersecting volumes

length: 21 meters (69 feet), width: 14.50 meters (48 feet), maximum height: 14 meters (46 feet), air pressure: 30–100 kilograms/square meter (14.73–14.83 pounds/square inch)

synthetic fabric, wire ropes

(in collaboration with Romberg)

page 91

While Frei Otto succeeded in building numerous tent structures, hardly any of his pneumatic membranes were executed. The test laboratory was one of the exceptions, demonstrating that certain functional and economic requirements could best be served with a membrane of composite form. The high-voltage laboratory has been enclosed in a double-domed membrane formed by two intersecting three-quarter spheres, which are tied down transversely where they connect by a restraining wire rope. An entrance tunnel with double doors provides the necessary air lock to preserve the internal pressure.

**Missile Installation Cover
Research Project 1959**

ellipsoidal pneumatic membrane
(in collaboration with Miles, Koch, Wehrhahn)
page 92

The project for a large factory for agricultural machinery shows the typical dome shape of a pneumatic membrane adapted to a rectangular plan, as well as the variations attainable by means of restraining wire ropes. A square two-story frame of administration offices and workshops functions as an abutment for the membrane, which covers a large assembly yard in the interior. Two heavily stressed cables subdivide the roof surface into four equal parts, reducing its overall height and its tension through the increase in curvature of each quadrant.

**Roof of a Factory for Agricultural Machinery
Research Project 1959**

pneumatic membrane over square plan with
2 axial restraining cables

lateral length: 200 meters (656 feet)

synthetic fabric externally coated (aluminum vapor),
wire ropes

(in collaboration with Miles, Koch, Wehrhahn)

page 93

**Offshore Storage Facility
Research Project 1958/1959**

pneumatic membrane over rectangular plan with
11 transverse restraining cables

synthetic fabric, wire ropes

(in collaboration with Development Center for
Lightweight Construction, Berlin)

page 93

The greenhouse envelope represents one of the most compelling images in Frei Otto's work, almost implying the conservation of nature against a destructive man-made climate. However utopian, the enormous pneumatic membrane is quite realizable and economical for agricultural purposes. Its size, permitting the growth of trees and use of machinery, renders the structure effective, since the amount of enclosed air virtually acts as a heat trap, retaining daytime irradiation which is not offset by air convection at night. The transparent, wire-rope-net-reinforced membrane is anchored at regular intervals where drainage pipes feed an overhead and underground irrigation system.

**Large-Scale Envelope for Agricultural Use
Research Project 1959**

high-and-low-point pneumatic membrane with
internal restraint points at regular intervals

maximum possible height: 20 meters (66 feet)

transparent, wire-rope-reinforced, synthetic fabric,
internal drainage and irrigation tubes

(in collaboration with Miles, Koch, Wehrhahn)

pages 94, 95

Convention and Exhibition Hall
Chicago, Illinois
Research Project (Yale University) 1960

high-and-low-point pneumatic membrane with central dome and 63 interior restraint points

lateral length: 300 meters (984 feet), dome span: 200 meters (656 feet), dome height: 45 meters (148 feet), low-point intervals: 25 meters (82 feet)

wire-reinforced, foam-insulated synthetic fabric

(in collaboration with Addiss, Kniffin, Childs)

pages 96, 97

From experiences with high-and-low-point tent structures, it was apparent that internal anchorages lowering parts of a membrane would consume less material and would reduce the stresses by introducing stronger curvatures between its low points. The scheme proposed a continuous pneumatic membrane over a hexagonal plan with a large dome at the center. The exhibition areas at the periphery of the dome were tied down at regular intervals creating funnel-shaped low points which also functioned as rainwater drains. With an average weight of 5 kilograms per square meter (12 ounces per square foot), the Convention Hall could be erected on land-fill in Lake Michigan.

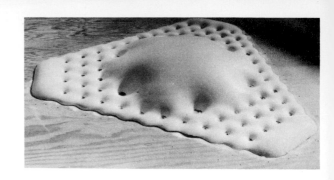

Oil Storage Tanks
Research Project 1959

continuous spherical membrane, either flexible (assuming its shape in the process of filling) or stabilized (maintaining its shape through pressure of displaceable gas)

high-strength, corrosion-resistant synthetic fabric

(in collaboration with Miles, Koch, Wehrhahn)

pages 98, 99

The spherical shape, basic to all pneumatic membranes, inspired numerous practical applications. Flattened mercury drops served as a model for continuous membranes which were developed as liquid containers. These storage tanks can be used either as flexible membranes which assume their shape in the process of filling, or they can be pre-stabilized through the pressure of a gas which is displaced in the process of filling. The containers are easily shipped as they can be folded up when empty.

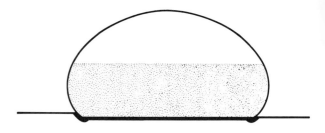

Roof for Exhibition Hall
Research Project 1959

pneumatic double membrane, triangular in plan, stressed between edge cables, and suspended at 3 points

maximum span: 40 meters (131 feet)

synthetic fabric, wire ropes, concrete abutments

(in collaboration with Miles, Koch, Wehrhahn)

page 98

Total enclosures by nature, pneumatic membranes can be employed as independent construction elements in the form of so-called cushions. In order to prevent these double membranes from bulging too strongly under their internal air pressure, they have to be heavily stressed outward on all sides by wire ropes, which, as in the case of this roof for an exhibition pavilion, need to be anchored in concrete abutments.

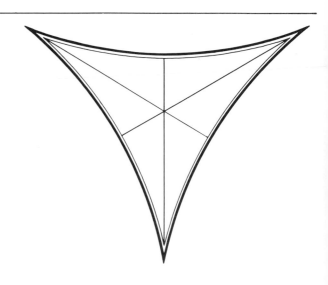

The exploration of potential applications of tensile structures was especially extensive in the field of pneumatic membranes. The typical drop shape of a membrane suspended at one point seemed most suited for grain, cement, and other granulated goods. The membranes, extended and reinforced at their tops, hang from tubular masts which contain the mechanics to charge and discharge their contents.

Silos for Grain or Cement
Research Project 1959

drop-like flexible membrane (assumes its shape in the process of filling) suspended from guyed mast (charge and discharge system in shaft of mast)

coated synthetic fabric, tubular steel masts, wire ropes

(in collaboration with Miles, Koch, Wehrhahn)

page 100

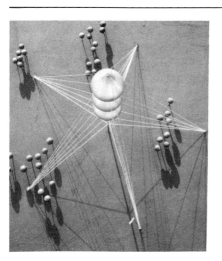

Water Tower
Research Project 1959

drop-like flexible membranes suspended from guyed mast, each attached to mast above its actual bottom level to relieve pressure (tanks interconnected to maintain equal water levels; charge and discharge system in shaft of mast)

height of mast: 40 meters (131 feet), diameter of tank: 8 meters (26 feet)

heavy synthetic fabric with imbedded wire mesh reinforcement, wire ropes, tubular steel mast

(in collaboration with Miles, Koch, Wehrhahn)

page 101

This so-called negative pneumatic structure was developed to provide concave surfaces for simultaneous projections of films and slides. The screen is formed by eight inwardly curved edge wire ropes delineating, at their connecting points, an oblong rectangular volume. Stretched between the cables is a coated fabric, which, due to the slight internal vacuum, is drawn in on all six sides producing the required curvatures. The screen, suspended in a metal frame, can be easily dismantled for use in another location.

Projection Screen
Industrial Fair
Berlin, Germany 1968

negative pneumatic membrane suspended between curved edge wire ropes, concave surfaces resulting from partial internal vacuum

length: 24 meters (79 feet), height: 12 meters (39 feet), negative (sub-atmospheric) internal pressure: 5 kilograms/square meter (0.007 pound/square inch)

synthetic fabric, wire ropes

(in collaboration with Romberg)

page 102

Chronology

1925
Born in Siegmar, Saxony

1952
Graduated in architecture at the Technological University, Berlin

1954
Doctoral thesis, "Das hängende Dach" ("The Suspended Roof")

1955
Bandstand, Federal Garden Exhibition, Kassel

1957
Founded Entwicklungsstätte für den Leichtbau (Development Center for Lightweight Construction), Berlin
Café Tents and Exhibition Hall, International Building Exhibition, Berlin
Dance Pavilion, Shelter Pavilion, Entrance Arch, Humped Pavilion, Federal Garden Exhibition, Cologne
Hangar tents mass-produced by L. Stromeyer and Company, Konstanz

1959
Pneumatic structures (research projects)

1960
Visiting Professor at Yale University, New Haven
Convention and Exhibition Hall, Chicago (research project at Yale)
Roof for Open-Air Theater, Nijmegen (project)

1961
Dock Cover, Bremen (project)

1962
Visiting Professor at the Technological University, Berlin and University of California, Berkeley
Lattice Dome Exhibition Structure, German Building Exhibition, Essen
Space frame structures (research project)
Published *Tensile Structures, Volume One: Pneumatic Structures*

1963
Wave Hall, Membrane Hall, Small Pavilions, International Horticultural Exhibition, Hamburg

1964
Professor at Technological University of Stuttgart
Founded Institut für leichte Flächentragwerke (Institute for Light Surface Structures), Technological

University of Stuttgart
Exhibition Pavilions, Swiss National Exhibition, Lausanne

1965
Roof for Terrace, Palm Beach Casino, Cannes
Construction Site Cover, North Peckham Redevelopment, Borough of Southwark, England (project)
Medical Academy, Ulm (project)

1966
High-Voltage Test Laboratory, Felten & Guilleaume Company, Cologne
Hotel and Conference Center, Riyadh (competition project)
Published *Tensile Structures, Volume Two: Cables, Nets and Membranes*

1967
Roof for Swimming Pool, Paris
Pavilion of the Federal Republic of Germany, World Exposition, Montreal
Indian Pavilion for World Exposition, Osaka (project)

1968
Roof for Open-Air Theater, Abbey Ruin, Bad Hersfeld

1969
Roofs for Sports Center Stadia, Kuwait (project)

1970
Roof for Olympic Stadium, Berlin (project)
Open-Air Theater, Wunsiedel

1971
Automatic Umbrella Roofs, Federal Garden Exhibition, Cologne

1972
Hotel and Conference Center, Mecca
Roofs for Olympic Stadia, Munich

Frei Otto's collaborators at the Development Center for Lightweight Construction in Berlin: A. Edzard, G. Gentsch, R. Krier, M. Lehmbrock, H. Redlich, U. Röder, B. F. Romberg, G. Scherzinger, R. v. Wild; at the Institute for Light Surface Structures and private office in Stuttgart: E. Asgeirson, E. Bubner, B. Burkhardt, F. Dressler, U. Hangleiter, E. Haug, J. Hennicke, C. Hesse, K. Keidel, F. Kiedaisch, M. Kreuz, R. Krier, F. Kugel, R. L. Medlin, G. Minke, J. Mirafuentes, F. Mohr, M. Morlock, B. Oleiko, B. Rasch, Jr., J. Schilling, J. Schock, J. Schoeller, H. Winter, G. Zwick.

Frei Otto on test structure for Stadia Roofs, Munich

Frei Otto's' own house, Warmbronn, completed 1970

Institute for Light Surface Structures, Stuttgart

Exhibition Structure

The exhibition shown at
The Museum of Modern Art, New York
from July 7 to October 4, 1971

was sponsored by

The Graham Foundation for Advanced Studies
in the Fine Arts, Chicago

with contributions by

Mrs. Douglas Auchincloss

D. S. and R. H. Gottesman Foundation

Konrad and Gabriele Henkel

Philip Johnson

Phyllis Lambert

Skidmore, Owings and Merrill

Thyssen Steel Corporation

Volkswagen of America

The exhibition structure was sponsored by

Farbwerke Hoechst, Frankfurt

with contributions by

the Foreign Office of the Federal Republic
of Germany

L. Stromeyer and Company, Konstanz

Exhibition Structure

The structure, initially designed as a retractable roof, was specially developed for the exhibition. It demonstrates the structural and formal potential of lightweight systems rather than their economical advantages, which are fully effective only at a larger scale. The structure, 64 feet long and 36 feet wide, demonstrates the separation of primary supporting members from the secondary enclosure system. The steel lattice masts (forming a 50-foot-high inverted V), the suspension wire ropes, and the anchor foundations provide an independently stable network against which the membrane is prestressed. Symmetrical along its major axis, the membrane —made of a translucent synthetic fabric—has a slightly inclined dome shape with a low frontal extension. The dome consists of simple saddle shapes, four in the higher, seven in the lower level; these are offset against each other at 90 degrees and joined along common cable-reinforced ridges. The outward apexes of the saddle segments are connected with eight radial suspension cables, while the inward apexes (with the exception of those at the highest point) are attached to a restraining cable encircling the interior. The extension of the main membrane over the stairs to the Sculpture Garden terrace is stabilized at two points by subsidiary masts. Its design was prompted by the site, but the entire structure can readily be re-erected on plane ground, proving the versatility and adaptability of these tensile systems.

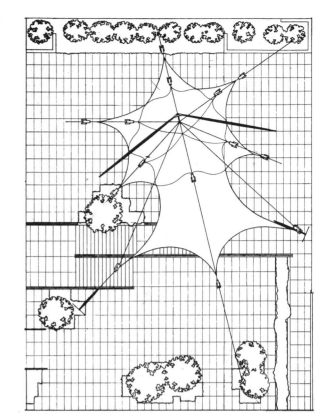

The exhibition structure was developed at the Lightweight Construction Center, Washington University, St. Louis, by its director, Richard Larry Medlin, in collaboration with Joachim Schoeller, Project Coordinator, and Dennis Bolazina, John Mike Cohen, John Fotsch, Edward Hord, William Hovland, Daniel Lemberg, Jan Peterson, and Douglas Tachi. It was manufactured in Germany by L. Stromeyer and Company, Konstanz, and erected in New York by John Gallin and Son and Heydt Contracting Corporation. The consulting engineer for the site preparation was John Zoldos, New York, and the architectural consultant for the erection was Thomas Lowrie, New York. The erection coordinator in the Museum was Matthew Donepp.

The synthetic fiber used for the exhibition structure, Trevira High Tenacity, was produced by Farbwerke Hoechst A.G., Frankfurt (United States distributor, Hystron Fibers, Inc., New York), and has been used for other projects by Frei Otto such as: the German Pavilion, Montreal; terrace roof, Cannes; open-air theater roof, Bad Hersfeld; swimming pool roofs, Paris and Lyons; automatic umbrella roofs, Cologne; open-air theater, Wunsiedel; projection screen, Berlin.

the work of frei otto